Carl
Sagan

Read These Other
Ferguson Career Biographies

Maya Angelou
Author and
Documentary Filmmaker
by Lucia Raatma

Leonard Bernstein
Composer and Conductor
by Jean F. Blashfield

Shirley Temple Black
Actor and Diplomat
by Jean F. Blashfield

George Bush
Business Executive
and U.S. President
by Robert Green

Bill Gates
Computer Programmer
and Entrepreneur
by Lucia Raatma

John Glenn
Astronaut and U.S. Senator
by Robert Green

Martin Luther King Jr.
Minister and
Civil Rights Activist
by Brendan January

Charles Lindbergh
Pilot
by Lucia Raatma

Sandra Day O'Connor
Lawyer and
Supreme Court Justice
by Jean Kinney Williams

Wilma Rudolph
Athlete and Educator
by Alice K. Flanagan

Carl
Sagan

Astronomer

JEAN F. BLASHFIELD

Ferguson Publishing Company
Chicago, Illinois

Photographs ©: Estate of Carl Sagan, cover; Monitor/Archive Photos, 8; International Feature Service/Hulton Getty/Liaison Agency, 11; A. E. French/Hulton Getty/Archive Photos, 13; Hulton Getty/Liaison Agency, 15; Paul J. Woolf/Hulton Getty/Archive Photos, 16; American Stock/Hulton Getty/Archive Photos, 19; AP/Wide World Photos, 21; Archive Photos, 24; AP/Wide World Photos, 25; Archive Photos, 27; Santi Visalli, Inc./Archive Photos, 31; UPI/Bettmann/Corbis, 33; Hulton Getty/Liaison Agency, 35; AP/Wide World Photos, 38, 43, 45; NASA, 48; James D. Wilson/Liaison Agency, 49; Jean P. Charbonnier/Rapho/Liaison Agency, 52; Steve Liss/Liaison Agency, 54; Archive Photos, 57; NASA, 60; Claudio Edinger/Liaison Agency, 62; Raphael Gaillarde/Liaison Agency, 65; AP/Wide World Photos, 68; Hulton Getty/Liaison, 71; Eduardo Castaneda/AP/Wide World Photos, 75; Monitor/Archive Photos, 80; UPI/Bettmann/Corbis, 82; Judy Sloan/Liaison Agency, 86; Liaison Agency, 91; Hulton Getty/Liaison Agency, 93; Karine Weinberger/Liaison Agency, 97; UPI/Bettmann/Corbis, 99; AP/Wide World Photos, 102; Michael J. Okoniewski/Liaison Agency, 105.

An Editorial Directions Book

Library of Congress Cataloging-in-Publication Data
Blashfield, Jean F.
    Carl Sagan : astronomer / by Jean F. Blashfield.
    p. cm.—(Ferguson career biographies)
    Includes bibliographical references and index.
    ISBN 0-89434-374-2
    1. Sagan, Carl, 1934—Juvenile literature. 2. Astronomers—United States—Biography—Juvenile literature. [1. Sagan, Carl, 1934– . 2. Astronomers.] I. Title. II. Series.

QB36.S15 B57 2001
520'.92—dc21
[B]   00-067264

Copyright © 2001 by Ferguson Publishing Company
Published and distributed by
Ferguson Publishing Company
200 West Jackson Boulevard, Suite 700
Chicago, Illinois 60606
www.fergpubco.com

Printed in the United States of America
Y-3

CONTENTS

Carl
Sagan

A remarkable scientist. Carl Sagan taught the world about life on Earth as well as in space.

THE "WONDER BUTTON"

I f you asked people in the late twentieth century to name a scientist, most of them would answer "Albert Einstein." In 1915, Einstein, a German scientist, developed the theory of relativity, which became the basis of modern astronomy and physics. But if you asked the same people to name a *living* scientist, they would certainly have answered "Carl Sagan."

Astronomers are often described as scientists who study the stars, but Carl Sagan was most interested in planets, such as Earth, and the reasons that life might develop on some but not on others. He was just as interested, though, in helping the public understand and appreciate science. And he did that better than anyone else.

To a New World

Sagan's grandfather came to the United States from what is now Ukraine in 1904. Leib Gruber (he later changed his name to Louis) had to leave his wife behind while he earned money for her passage to America. She came the following year and gave birth to Rachel, Carl's mother, some months later.

Rachel's mother died the following year when Rachel's sister was born. Gruber sent Rachel back to Europe to be taken care of by an aunt. Fortunately, Gruber soon married again and was able to bring Rachel back to the United States. These experiences, however, left Rachel feeling unsettled. She became a demanding, exuberant, lively, and very bright woman who wanted to go to college and even wanted to work—both unusual ambitions in those years.

Carl's other grandfather also came from what would later be the Soviet Union. After his wife died in childbirth, he left for the United States. In 1910, his son Samuel was brought by an uncle to join him. In New York City, young Samuel Sagan began to dream of a better future. He was about to go to university to study to become a pharmacist when the stock market crashed in 1929. The world entered a severe economic depression. Samuel was forced to drop out of college.

New York City in 1925. Samuel Sagan moved here before meeting and marrying Rachel Gruber.

Samuel was working as an usher in a movie theater when he met Rachel Gruber. Forgetting his earlier goals, he took a job with the New York Girl Coat Company, which his uncle had started. Samuel would work for the coat company for the rest of his life.

Little Carl

The two Jewish families from the Soviet Union were united in 1933 when Rachel and Samuel married. Their first child, Carl Edward, was born on November 9, 1934. Carl inherited equal portions of two attitudes: skepticism, or doubt about everything, from his mother, and optimism from his father. But Rachel's skepticism was never focused on Carl. She was certain he was the brightest, handsomest boy in the world, and she always told him so. The ambition Rachel once had for herself, she transferred to her son.

The family lived in an apartment in Brooklyn, not far from the Atlantic Ocean. They could walk to Coney Island, a big beach and amusement park. Another advantage of living in Brooklyn was the many museums, art galleries, and concert halls in nearby Manhattan. Both Rachel and Samuel

Coney Island in 1935. Young Carl Sagan grew up in a part of Brooklyn that was very close to this beach and amusement park.

believed in exposing their children to as many cultural experiences as possible. Carl was particularly fascinated by the star shows at the Hayden Planetarium at the American Museum of Natural History.

In 1939, New York City ignored the growing war in Europe that would become World War II (1939–1945). The city hosted a huge celebration called the New York World's Fair. The theme for the fair was the future, the "World of Tomorrow." Carl, taken several times to see the fair, found it very exciting to think that he was going to live in a future that was so technologically advanced.

The Sagan family paid little attention to World War II during Carl's childhood. They knew that their relatives in Europe were probably in danger—perhaps already dead—just because they were Jewish, but the family didn't talk about it. Rachel wanted to nourish the optimistic portion of Carl's personality.

Seemingly from birth, Carl had what his sister Cari (born when he was seven) later called his "wonder button." He would see something new and start wondering about it. Sagan's "wonder button" was often pressed when he was a child, and it continued to function throughout his life.

His parents encouraged him to consider all possibilities when thinking about what he was going to do when he grew up. They never tried to direct him in one way or another, except to assume that he would get a college education, which could take him anywhere. All they asked was that he care about what he did.

The planetarium, the books, and the "wonder button" all played a part in giving Carl an ambition.

The World of Tomorrow. Young Carl was intrigued by all he saw at the 1939 World's Fair.

The "Wonder Button"

Years later, he told an interviewer, "Since childhood, the most pleasurable occupation I could imagine was being a scientist. It had a romance to it that nothing else I know of even approached. And I've never lost that. . . . I actually have spent much of the last thirty-five years exploring the solar system of my childhood dream."

The Hayden Planetarium. As a boy, Carl Sagan enjoyed the star shows he watched here.

Predicting the Future

Sagan loved to tell two incidents from his childhood, incidents that predicted his future. In the first one, he had been wondering about those little lights in the sky that people called stars. When he asked adults what they were, he got no good answer, so he went to the library and asked for a book on stars. The librarian, seeing a slight young child standing before her, assumed that he was asking about Hollywood stars. To his disgust, she gave him a book filled with pictures of famous movie actors and actresses. Carl finally made the librarian understand that he meant the stars in the sky. She found the right book, and soon he was discovering that those lights in the sky were actually suns like the one he saw every day. Even then, he wondered if those suns had planets like Earth around them.

In the second incident, Carl was about twelve and was visiting his grandfather Gruber, who asked Carl (through a translator because he had never learned English) what he wanted to be when he grew up. Carl replied that he thought he wanted to be an astronomer, a person who studies the stars. "Yes," his grandfather said, "but how will you earn a living?"

Carl, seeing his father go off to a rather boring job every day, supposed that he would have to do some similar work. But he would play at being an astronomer on weekends and at night.

The Fictional World

The real universe fascinated Carl but, at age ten, he discovered the fictional universe, which he found equally fascinating. He liked *Superman* and other comics, but he soon found that he liked the science-fiction Martian novels of Edgar Rice Burroughs even more. Today, Burroughs is best known for his *Tarzan of the Apes*, but in the 1940s, he was equally popular for his John Carter novels. The character of John Carter was a Confederate soldier who had become a "gentleman explorer." Carter traveled to Mars, Venus, and other planets, though how he did this was never quite explained.

Even at that age, Carl knew that most of the science in Burroughs's novels wasn't really science, but that didn't matter. The novels and the science-fiction magazines he later discovered fed his dreams about exploring the solar system.

Soon after the war ended in 1945, the Sagan coat factory opened a new plant in Perth Amboy, New

Edgar Rice Burroughs. This author was known for science fiction as well as his Tarzan novels.

Jersey. Samuel Sagan became the manager, and he moved his family to nearby Rahway. In 1948, Carl started high school at the age of thirteen—he had skipped two grades.

It was in Rahway that Carl learned he could consider becoming an astronomer after all. In his sophomore year, he was astonished when his science teacher told Carl that astronomers actually got paid, usually by universities, to do their work. Carl no longer had any doubts about where he was heading.

During high school, Carl acquired a book called *Interplanetary Flight.* An English author named Arthur C. Clarke wrote it. Carl was gripped by Clarke's explanations of how rockets could actually travel out into space. He couldn't have dreamed that he and that same Arthur C. Clarke would later become good friends.

Carl was never a popular boy. He was too bright—and too willing to show that he was bright—for popularity. When teachers at Rahway High School realized just how bright he was, they encouraged his parents to send him to a private school for intelligent children. Samuel and Rachel chose not to, perhaps because of the cost. They did, however,

Arthur C. Clarke. Carl Sagan enjoyed Clarke's writing, and eventually the two men became friends.

see that he had a bar mitzvah (a Jewish coming-of-age ceremony) when he was thirteen. But thereafter Carl never made religion a part of his life.

Although he was a bit of a "loner," Carl participated in many school activities, such as the chemistry club, the French club, the Debating Society, the school newspaper, and the drama group. He didn't shy away from sports either, though his only skill was keeping team statistics. Once he reached 6 feet 2 inches (188 centimeters), though, he was welcome on the basketball court. He also became an excellent pianist who delighted in playing for others. His mother thought he might become a concert pianist, but Carl's ambitions were in a quite different direction.

Heading for College

In June 1951, Carl Sagan graduated from high school and prepared to leave home. Despite the appeal of an eastern Ivy League college such as Princeton University, Carl was more attracted to the University of Chicago. That school on the south side of Chicago proudly proclaimed that it didn't have a football team or an active fraternity. All it offered him was a good solid education and scholarships to go there.

Carl Sagan was only sixteen, two years younger than most freshmen, when he arrived at the University of Chicago. At that time, the university still featured an educational program that gave every student, regardless of his or her interests, a solid grounding in the classics. They studied the Greek writers, the original works of such great scientists as Sir Isaac Newton, and the Latin classics. Students had to earn a bachelor's degree in liberal arts before they could concentrate on anything else. When Sagan started writing, he was very glad for the liberal arts education he received at the University of Chicago.

Making Connections

Carl was never shy about approaching the people who had answers he wanted, no matter how illustrious those people were. During his university years, Sagan got to know several scientists who would play a role in his career.

The first one was Hermann J. Muller, an important scientist working in the new field of genetics at the University of Indiana. He had won the 1946 Nobel Prize in physiology and medicine for discovering that X rays could causes changes in a person's genes. Such changes might have played a role in evolution.

Carl became friends with one of the graduate students working with Muller. The Indiana student invited Carl to visit him in Bloomington, Indiana, and introduced him to Dr. Muller. Muller liked Carl

Hermann J. Muller. This scientist offered Sagan a job in his laboratory one summer.

and offered him a summer job in his laboratory, which he gladly accepted.

It was not a fun job—he had to make sure that fruit flies were separated into males and females right after they hatched. (Fruit flies are used in genetics experiments because they have a very short life cycle.) It was meticulous and rather boring work, but Carl and Dr. Muller spent a great deal of time discussing other things. A favorite topic was extraterrestrial life—life on other planets. The search for extraterrestrial intelligence (SETI) would engage Sagan for many years to come.

After a long day in the laboratory, Carl went out to search the skies. At that time, he wasn't looking at stars—he was hoping to see flying saucers. Then, as now, unidentified flying objects, or UFOs, were a popular subject.

UFOs over Salem, Massachusetts. Sagan often spent time watching the skies for such objects.

Chemical Soup

Another scientist who had an influence on Sagan, especially in regard to the origin of life, was Harold Clayton Urey, a chemist at the University of Chicago. He had won the 1934 Nobel Prize in chemistry for his discovery of a form of hydrogen called deuterium.

In regular hydrogen, only a single proton, or positively charged particle, makes up the nucleus of the atom. Deuterium has a proton *plus* a non-charged particle, which is called a neutron. Urey also helped to develop the atomic bomb that ended World War II.

Muller introduced Sagan to Urey because Urey had recently become interested in the chemistry of life. Urey and a graduate student named Stanley Miller were testing the idea that in the early history of the planet a soupy mixture of chemicals was changed by lightning into organic compounds. (To a chemist, *organic* means that the molecules contain carbon.) All living things are made of a complex variety of organic compounds.

Astonishingly, the Miller-Urey experiment produced amino acids—compounds that are basic to life. Science writer Isaac Asimov wrote, "If in one

Harold Urey. This scientist won the 1934 Nobel Prize in chemistry and had great influence on Sagan.

week, and in one small setup, Miller could get amino acids, how much could be done in a billion years?" Sagan thought Miller's results demonstrated that life could happen anywhere in the universe, not only on Earth.

Reaching for Degrees

Sagan wrote about his ideas on the origins of life for his senior honors paper, a project that is called a thesis. He graduated with his bachelor of arts honors degree and was finally ready to concentrate on science. But instead of diving right into astronomy, he chose physics. He earned a bachelor of science degree in 1955 and a master of science degree in 1956.

At the same time, he acquired a girlfriend, a young woman named Lynn Alexander. She was so bright that she had transferred to the university directly from her sophomore year in high school. Soon Sagan and Alexander's relationship grew serious, and they began talking marriage.

Even though Carl was concentrating on physics, the first scientific paper he published dealt with life in the universe. Published in the journal *Evolution,* it was called "Radiation and the Origin of the Gene." It did not report research. Instead, it reviewed the work of other scientists. Eventually, Carl Sagan would publish more than 500 articles in scientific journals.

He was finally ready to become an astronomer.

At Cornell. Carl Sagan became a professor at Cornell after leaving Harvard University.

THE YOUNG ASTRONOMER

n 1956, Sagan was accepted by the University of Chicago's graduate school of astronomy, which was located at Yerkes Observatory in Williams Bay, Wisconsin, a tiny town on Lake Geneva, just across the border from Illinois. Yerkes, home of the world's largest refracting telescope, is known for the important scientific work done there. The director of the observatory was Dr. Gerard Kuiper, one of the few astronomers who studied planets.

To find out more about the work of an astronomer, Sagan decided to accept Dr.

Kuiper's invitation to spend the summer working at McDonald Observatory in Fort Davis, Texas. During that summer, Mars was closer to Earth than it had been for many years—or would be again for a long time. Even so, Sagan's first view of the mysterious planet through a large telescope was very disappointing. It looked like a distant yellowish disk, not at all like the exciting place Edgar Rice Burroughs had written about.

Lively Mars

Sagan looked forward to learning from Indian-born astrophysicist Subrahmanyan Chandrasekhar. Chandrasekhar shared the 1983 Nobel Prize in physics, for research on the evolution and death of stars. But Sagan's natural curiosity about planets and the possibilities of life on them drew him to work more closely with Dr. Kuiper.

Gerard Kuiper believed there was life on Mars, as did many astronomers. The planet was known to have areas of darkness that expanded during part of the year and shrank back later. Kuiper was certain that the changes were caused by vegetation that grew and expanded and then died.

Part of the reason Kuiper was so certain of Mar-

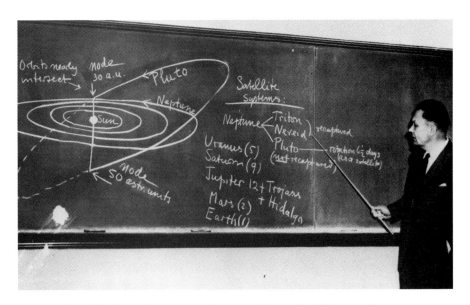

Gerard Kuiper. Sagan was drawn to the work of this noted scientist at the Yerkes Observatory.

tian life was that an instrument called a spectroscope showed that the gas carbon dioxide was present in the planet's thin atmosphere. Carbon dioxide is the gas that Earth's plants must have in order for photosynthesis (food production in green plants) to take place. Plants take in carbon dioxide and give out oxygen, while animals take in oxygen and give out carbon dioxide.

At that time, there was no way to get solid information about the planets. Studying them was guesswork. Kuiper guessed that there was water on the planet for plants to use. He *wanted* the changing dark areas on Mars to be living plants.

But Sagan wasn't so sure. Like Kuiper, he wanted to verify life on Mars, but Sagan thought the dark areas were more likely to be dark rocks, such as lava, that were sometimes covered by light-colored sand. Mars was known to have major windstorms, so it seemed reasonable to Sagan that sand or dust could be blown around.

In December 1956, at age twenty-two, Sagan delivered his first scientific paper to a meeting of the Society for the Study of Evolution, which was held during the annual meeting of the American Association for the Advancement of Science (AAAS). He described his analysis of Mars's "seasonal changes," disagreeing with Dr. Kuiper's thinking.

At Home and in Space

Carl Sagan and Lynn Alexander were married in June 1957. She was only nineteen and still in school herself. She started graduate school at the University of Wisconsin in Madison, and Sagan—glad to get out of little Williams Bay—commuted the 60 miles (97 kilometers) from Madison to the observatory.

Explorer *in January 1958. This satellite launch was the start of the U.S. race into space.*

The world was stunned when, on October 4, 1957, it was announced that the Soviet Union had put *Sputnik*, the world's first artificial satellite, into orbit around Earth. Several months later, on January 31, 1958, the first successful U.S. satellite was launched. The space race between the United States and the Soviet Union had begun. It was more about politics and showmanship than it was about science, but it was an exciting time to be in planetary astronomy.

Carl's mind was so thoroughly out in space that he was unwilling to take time to do household tasks to help Lynn, not even after their first son, Dorion, was born in 1959. Lynn became concerned that she could not take care of Carl and Dorion and work on her graduate studies in biology. When a second son, Jeremy, was born the following year, life became even harder for Carl Sagan's wife.

Protecting the Planets

In Madison, Sagan got to know Dr. Joshua Lederberg, a professor at the University of Wisconsin. Lederberg, shaken by the Soviet Union's first satellite, became concerned about the impact of humans venturing into space. He worried that Earthlings might contaminate the moon. However, U.S. officials paid no attention to his concerns, despite the fact that he was a Nobel Prize winner. He had earned his 1958 prize for using bacteria to change the genetic makeup of living things.

Sagan was an astronomer and Lederberg was a geneticist. Together, the two shared their knowledge and delighted in speculating about life in the universe. Lederberg would later be credited with creating the term *exobiology*, the study of life beyond Earth. However, Carl Sagan was truly the first exobiologist.

Sagan soon published two articles that pursued the possibility of contaminating the moon with Earth-life. Combined with Lederberg's earlier letters, the articles forced officials in the U.S. government to consider the problem. Both the United States and the Soviet Union then incorporated sterilization procedures into their plans for launching spacecraft.

His growing reputation put Sagan in the public eye. He became one of the people consulted by agencies, universities, and organizations involved in space exploration and one who was asked questions about planets and life in the universe. Some of the jobs were—and are—top secret.

More Organic Soup

After Dorion was born, the Sagans spent the summer at the University of California at Berkeley. Carl worked in the laboratory of Melvin Calvin, a biologist who won a Nobel Prize in 1961. Sagan learned to use an instrument called an infrared spectrometer to search for organic molecules.

Sagan and Stanley Miller, who had worked with Urey, developed "soups" of organic molecules and put an electric charge through them. Sagan then used his new skill to measure the results. He created a chart of organic molecules that he could use for comparing spectrometer readings from the planets, such as from Jupiter, where he hoped to find such molecules in the atmosphere.

The paper Sagan and Miller wrote on this work for the *Astronomical Journal* attracted public attention. Reporters interpreted the paper to mean that living things were floating around in the atmosphere of Jupiter. They mostly got it wrong, and Carl Sagan began to realize how important it was that the public understand enough science to comprehend what was happening in their world. He would spend the remainder of his life working toward that goal.

Biologist Melvin Calvin. Sagan worked in Calvin's laboratory and learned to use an infrared spectrometer.

The Venus Study

Carl Sagan earned his Ph.D. in astronomy and physics in 1960 with a study called simply "Physical Studies of Planets." A large part of his work had to do with the planet Venus. He expanded this material into an article that appeared in *Science,* one of the world's most influential science journals. Called "The Planet Venus," it was published in March 1961.

Most people then believed that Venus, like Mars, was a "sister planet" very like Earth. But Sagan said that it was highly unlikely that life could exist on Venus. He explained that even what was known about the planet from long distance showed that the extra-dense atmosphere contained molecules, especially carbon dioxide, that would produce a greenhouse effect, similar to the one that keeps Earth warm, but much more powerful.

Sunlight goes through the atmosphere and strikes a planet's surface, where light rays change into heat radiation. On planets without atmosphere, the heat is radiated right back into space. On planets with an atmosphere, however, molecules can trap the radiation, holding it close to the surface. This is called the greenhouse effect because the atmosphere acts like the glass in a greenhouse, trapping heat. Since Venus has such a thick atmosphere of carbon dioxide, Sagan proposed that Venus probably had a very high temperature. Even in this heavily scientific article, Sagan's skill with language and poetic notions of the universe were evident.

In a flamboyant addition to the article, Sagan proposed that perhaps Earthlings could change Venus to make it more habitable, or "terraform" it, meaning transform it into an Earthlike place.

These changes could be made by dropping plant microbes, such as algae, into Venus's atmosphere. These primitive green plants could then carry out photosynthesis as they do on Earth. They would take carbon dioxide and water vapor from the atmosphere and convert it into oxygen and other chemicals, gradually changing Venus into a planet where Earthlings could live. (It was later found that Venus also has vast quantities of sulfuric acid in its atmosphere, so Sagan's terraforming plan wouldn't have worked.)

As had happened earlier, prominent newspapers such as the *New York Times* picked up Sagan's idea and turned it into headlines that caught the imagination of the public. His description of Venus was later picked up by environmentalists. They see

Venus as an example of what Earth could become if something isn't done to slow global warming.

NASA Calls

After earning his doctorate, Sagan took his family back to California. There he worked at the Institute for Basic Research in Science at the University of California at Berkeley for two years. And he continued his search for extraterrestrial life.

The Soviet Union put the first human into space in 1961, when the United States had barely succeeded in launching a satellite. But the National Aeronautics and Space Agency (NASA) already had dreams about exploring the solar system.

Carl Sagan was invited to go to NASA's Jet Propulsion Laboratory in Pasadena to consult on plans for sending a probe called Mariner to fly past Venus. Some of the scientists involved wanted to leave cameras off the craft so that other instruments could go on. Sagan tried to convince them that there were things worth photographing and the public would want to see pictures. But he lost the argument. He worked on developing radiometers, instruments to measure radiation. The measurements taken by one kind of radiometer on board would

Checking Mariner 1. *This craft was sent to explore Venus in 1962.*

The Young Astronomer

prove or disprove his own published speculations about Venus.

Because of its record of rocket failures, NASA planned to launch two Mariner spacecraft toward Venus. *Mariner 1* was launched on July 22, 1962, but

Mariner 2 *on its way to Venus. This craft was launched five weeks after the* Mariner 1.

it had to be destroyed because the rocket went off course. Five weeks later, *Mariner 2* was successfully launched through Earth's atmosphere. The small probe was on its way to Venus, almost 200 million miles (322 million km) away. *Mariner 2* arrived in the vicinity of Venus in December 1962. The gravitational pull of the planet drew the probe toward it for a brief thirty-five minutes, as the instruments aboard did their work.

The flyby was a total success for Sagan. The instruments showed that his speculations were probably right. Venus was very hot indeed, even hotter than Sagan had projected.

While *Mariner 2* was on its way to Venus, Carl and Lynn were divorced. She later earned her own doctorate in biology and, as Lynn Margulis, became known as one of the most influential scientists in the United States. Ultimately, their son Dorion would write books of his own, including some written with his mother.

After dealing with information from the Venus flyby, Sagan—distressed by the failure of his marriage—went to Harvard University to begin his work there as an assistant professor. He remained in Cambridge, Massachusetts, for six years.

The Editor

In 1962, several astronomers started a new scientific journal called *Icarus,* which was intended to concentrate on studies of the solar system. They immediately asked Sagan if he would like to be an associate editor. One of the skills he needed in the job was the ability to recognize valid ideas and to suggest new approaches or possible criticisms. Sagan's broad knowledge and insight came in very handy. In 1968, Sagan became editor of *Icarus,* a position he held for more than a decade.

Ultimately, about half of Sagan's books were created while he was the editor of *Icarus*, working with the essays and studies of many different researchers. He was able to draw the best out of other people and to bring together ideas from many different sources.

Mars and the Moon

Having looked at Venus, both Sagan and NASA turned their attention to Earth's other neighbor—Mars. The young Dr. Sagan led a number of conferences at which scientists discussed the red planet, mostly with speculations about life on Mars and how to explore it safely. At that time, most Americans assumed that humans would soon stand on Mars.

Work began on Martian Mariner probes. *Mariner 4*—carrying a camera—was launched on November 28, 1964. The following July 14, its orbit carried it to within about 6,000 miles (9,654 km) of the planet. The first "close-up" photos were transmitted immediately back to Earth, where they were a huge disappointment. A dry, crater-marked surface showed no signs of living things.

In the face of many discouraged newspaper articles, Sagan pointed out that from 6,000 miles (9,654 km) up there's no sign of life on Earth either! But even NASA was disappointed and canceled plans for a probe that would land on the surface of Mars.

For some years, Carl Sagan was one of the few advocates of more missions to Mars. He co-wrote the Time-Life book *Planets* as part of his advocacy. He talked on numerous television shows and wrote popular articles for *National Geographic*.

Both NASA's and the public's attention now focused on Apollo missions to land men on the moon—a program that President John F. Kennedy had called for. When the first moon rocks were

The team of Apollo 11. *The crew members were (left to right) Neil Armstrong, Michael Collins, and Edwin Aldrin.*

brought back to Earth by the astronauts of *Apollo 11* in 1969, Sagan was able to study samples through a scanning electron microscope. There was no sign that even the tiniest bacterium had ever lived there.

SETI

Dr. Frank Drake at the National Radio Astronomy Observatory in Green Bank, West Virginia, suggested using small radiotelescope to search for radio signals that might indicate the existence of life beyond Earth. Such signals would have a pattern to them that did not occur in the mixed-up collection of signals that come naturally from sources all over the universe.

Drake called his brief 1960 search Project Ozma. As he explained in his memoirs *Is Anyone Out There?: The Search for Extraterrestrial Intelligence,* the name was "for the princess of the imaginary land of Oz—a place very far away, difficult to reach, and populated by exotic beings." All Ozma did was tune into one radio frequency and focus on two stars for a period of two weeks. It was much too small to be a test, but it was a beginning for the search for extraterrestrial intelligence.

In 1961 Carl Sagan was the youngest person invited to a conference at Green Bank. The attending scientists discussed where to go next with SETI, how to improve their chances of receiving signals from intelligent aliens. Years later, Sagan exclaimed how wonderful it had been to have "these good

Dr. Francis Drake. His work made progress in the search for extraterrestrial intelligence.

scientists all saying that it wasn't nonsense to think about" receiving signals from an alien civilization.

Then a Russian radioastronomer named I. S. Shklovskii came to Sagan's attention because he had been proposing—in a book published in the stiff, stern, unimaginative Soviet Union—the possibility that the moons of Mars were artificial space stations, perhaps launched long ago by a vanished Martian society. It was just the kind of outrageous idea that Sagan loved. The Russian and the American became long-distance friends.

Sagan persuaded Shklovskii to let him prepare an edition of the book for the U.S. market that would include Sagan's own comments. In 1966, Sagan published their joint book as *Intelligent Life in the Universe*. It was a popular treatment of a complicated subject, told with wit and the power to fascinate. Like a conversation, it alternated smoothly between Shklovskii's heavy science and Soviet politics, and Sagan's lighter approach. Perhaps most exciting was the idea that a Soviet scientist and an American scientist, at the height of the Cold War, could work together.

In the meantime, science-fiction writer Arthur C. Clarke and filmmaker Stanley Kubrick were

On the set. Stanley Kubrick directed the 1968 film 2001: A Space Odyssey.

Carl Sagan: Astronomer

planning a movie called *Journey Beyond the Stars*. In the mid-1960s, Clarke, who was already a friend of Sagan's, called him in as a consultant. Clarke and Kubrick were arguing about what the extraterrestrials who appear at the end of the movie should look like—humanlike or totally alien. They wanted Sagan's opinion.

Sagan said that there was no way that a humanlike being could ever evolve except in an Earthlike time and place. In the end, film was made with just lights and sounds indicating an extraterrestrial intelligence. It was released in 1968 as *2001: A Space Odyssey*.

From Harvard to Cornell

While all this was going on, Sagan was teaching at Harvard University. He also supervised the work of graduate students, many of whom later became important in astronomy and the space program. He also met Linda Salzman, a bright young student from Tufts University.

Professors at Harvard had often looked down on the flamboyant Sagan. Perhaps they were jealous of the public attention he got. Some of them undoubtedly thought he didn't spend enough time

In front of the class. Sagan was appreciated and praised by the students and administration at Cornell University.

on "serious" astronomy. Whatever the reasons, when it came time for Sagan to be given a permanent position at Harvard (called tenure), he was denied it.

Cornell University at Ithaca, New York, pursued Sagan, hoping to add him to their astronomy staff. Sagan was drawn to Ithaca because Frank Drake was already there and because Cornell controlled Arecibo, the world's largest radio telescope, located in Puerto Rico.

Carl and Linda were married as he was preparing to move to Ithaca. Unlike Harvard, Cornell enjoyed and celebrated Carl Sagan. He later became director of Cornell's Laboratory for Planetary Studies and was named the David Duncan Professor of Astronomy and Space Sciences. Being given a named professorship is a very high honor. Over the next twenty-five years, almost everything he did at Cornell brought him more fame.

A world away. Sagan supported and encouraged the exploration of life on Mars.

MARS HUNTER

I n November 1971, photographs taken by *Mariner 9* started coming from Mars to Earth. In the onboard equipment, photographs were translated into dots, rather like pixels on a computer monitor. Each dot was given measurements for position and darkness. These measurements were radioed back to Earth where a computer then reassembled the photos.

Taking advantage of the huge dust storm, the scientists at the Jet Propulsion Laboratory could radio instructions for the cameras to change direction. This allowed them to concentrate on four spots that had intrigued them but which were not on the planned agenda. Considerable work finally showed that these spots were huge volcanoes. One of them, Olympus Mons, is an incredible 15 miles (25 km) high, with a volume 100 times greater than the largest volcano on Earth.

When the dust storm cleared,the cameras did the work that had originally been planned—mapping the surface. At that time, they discovered a rift valley, a huge feature where two chunks of the planet's crust have moved apart. At 124 miles (200 km) wide and 2,486 miles (4,000 km) long, it is three times as deep as the Grand Canyon.

The most exciting thing from Sagan's point of view was that smaller channels near the rift looked like water-formed channels on Earth. Earlier Mariner spacecraft had already shown that there was no running water on Mars. But perhaps there had been water in the past.

Scientists theorized that perhaps Mars is now in a long "ice age," similar to those that occurred on Earth, and that any life that might once have been on the planet had gone into a hibernation, which has lasted thousands of years. This idea was part of the thinking behind the Viking mission planned for 1976.

Mariner 9 worked for almost a year, though it was planned for a mission of only ninety days. It sent more than 7,000 pictures of Mars back to Earth to be studied and interpreted. Even more pictures were taken but some were never returned to Earth. The craft is still in orbit around Mars. Perhaps one day it will be picked up by astronauts from Earth and the pictures will be seen.

Messages into Space

A spacecraft called *Pioneer 10* was launched on March 3, 1972, in a trajectory, or path, that would take it safely through the asteroids between Mars and Jupiter. At Jupiter, the gravity of the giant planet would give *Pioneer 10* enough additional velocity to send it beyond the far reaches of our solar system. Maybe many thousands of years from now, the small hunk of metal and plastic would be spotted by alien beings and retrieved.

A few months before launch, Sagan contacted NASA and suggested that some sort of message be put on the *Pioneer 10* spacecraft. NASA officials liked the idea, but they said that whatever form it took had to be quick and small. Sagan would later call the message the "first serious attempt to communicate with extraterrestrial civilizations."

He and Frank Drake, with help from Sagan's wife Linda, quickly created a message that was etched on a gold-plated aluminum plaque. At 6 by 9 inches (15 by 23 centimeters), it was light enough not to affect the launch or trajectory of the spacecraft. It was mounted on one of the struts that supported the antenna.

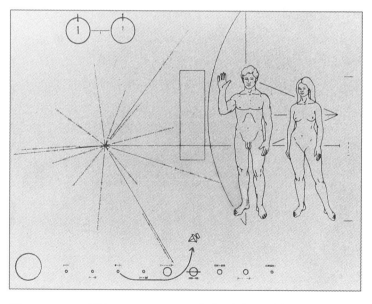

The message of Pioneer 10. *Sagan helped design this plaque that was carried into outer space.*

The message, Sagan said, is mostly science. It could be interpreted by any civilization that is at least as advanced as ours. The most puzzling part of the message would probably be the figures of naked male and female humans. Any civilization finding the spacecraft may not resemble humans at all. Newspapers and magazines all over the world showed the plaque. Editorials were written about it. People argued. Everyone had an opinion on how it should have been designed. Some people were shocked that it had naked humans on it. But by then Earth's message was on its way to the stars.

Reaching the Public

Jerome Agel, a TV and book producer as well as writer, shared with Sagan his concern that the public in general paid little attention to science. He asked Sagan to consider writing a book that would convey the excitement the astronomer felt about his work. Sagan agreed, and he dictated it into a portable recorder while crossing the country with his wife Linda and their son, Nicholas. The result was *The Cosmic Connection: An Extraterrestrial Perspective*, which was published in the fall of 1973.

He was able to incorporate everything he liked

most. He explained astrophysics to the general public, chatted about his childhood memories of reading Edgar Rice Burroughs, speculated on extraterrestrial life, philosophized on the meaning of life, debunked (disproved) unidentified flying objects as interstellar spaceships, and stressed the importance of space exploration.

After writer Isaac Asimov read Sagan's book, Asimov wrote him: "I have just finished *The Cosmic*

Isaac Asimov. This science-fiction writer was a big fan of Sagan's book The Cosmic Connection.

Connection and loved every word of it. You are my idea of a good writer because you have an unmannered style, and when I read what you write, I hear you talking. One thing about the book made me nervous. It was entirely too obvious that you are smarter than I am. I hate that."

Television Beckons

On November 30, 1973, Carl Sagan appeared on *The Tonight Show* with Johnny Carson, primarily as a result of *The Cosmic Connection.* He was supposed to explain what the space probes to other planets were all about. Carson and everyone else expected a rather dull explanation, to which they could nod and say thank-you. Instead, they were gripped by Sagan's dramatic story of new worlds. He sounded as if he knew the planets through personal experience.

Sagan had found a new way to share his excitement about planets and space with the public, and the public had found a new hero. The astronomer would return again and again to the late-night show. A large segment of the American population learned all they knew about astronomy from Carl Sagan on *The Tonight Show*.

Sagan and SETI

Sagan wrote in *The Cosmic Connection,* "We now have, for the first time, the tools to make contact with civilizations on planets of other stars. It is an astonishing fact that the great one-thousand-foot-diameter radiotelescope of the National Astronomy and Ionsophere Center, run by Cornell University in Arecibo, Puerto Rico, would be able to communicate with an identical copy of itself anywhere in the Milky Way Galaxy."

Sagan passionately backed all the SETI programs, and he would later be influential in persuading the government to provide funds for the search. Not because he was so certain that there was life out there somewhere, but because he knew it was worth the work and cost of finding out.

Oddly, Sagan himself participated in only one SETI activity during his career. He spent a few days during the summer of 1975 with Frank Drake at Arecibo Observatory in Puerto Rico. They aimed the receivers of the world's largest radiotelescope at chosen areas of the sky and settled back to watch electrical signals come in from outer space, appearing as lines on the monitor of an instrument. But Sagan didn't have the patience to sit there day after day

The world's largest radiotelescope. Cornell University operates this technology in Arecibo, Puerto Rico.

Mars Hunter

watching for changes in signals that never came. He left the watching and listening to others. He preferred to wonder and speculate.

In 1978, government funding of SETI won Wisconsin Senator William Proxmire's Golden Fleece Award for wasteful government spending. Sagan sat down with Proxmire and demonstrated to the Wisconsin senator that there were important benefits in the search. Proxmire was persuaded enough to let at least minimal funding go through.

Sagan later developed a petition that supported SETI and was signed by seventy-one important figures in science, including seven Nobel Prize winners. It was published in the October 1982 issue of *Science.* The following year, the U.S. government funded a five-year study of SETI. The SETI Institute, under the directorship of Frank Drake, was then established in California.

People often asked, "If there are intelligent aliens out there, why haven't they been in touch with us on Earth?" Sagan replied that if the aliens were warmongers, they were too busy killing one another to venture out into the universe. And if they were peaceable, they were using their skills at healing and helping the planets in their own vicinity.

The Viking Landers

The success of the *Mariner 9* mission made NASA start planning the Viking craft that was to land on Mars. Again, Sagan was involved in the work. Again, he didn't always get his own way. He had not given up hope that there might be some large form of life on the planet, and he wanted a camera that would be able to pick up movement. Choosing where to land the craft was an important part of the planning. Usually a place that looked safe for landing didn't look as if it might support life of any kind. The planning group argued continuously about the landing sites. The only thing that was certain was that NASA was aiming to have the first Viking land on Mars on July 4, 1976, the 200th birthday of the United States.

Despite all the debate, when *Viking 1* neared the planet and the first photos were sent back, the chosen landing site turned out to be a mass of rough land that would probably destroy the fragile craft. The Fourth of July landing had to be canceled while a new site was chosen and the computers reprogrammed. *Viking 1* eventually landed on July 20.

Experiments aimed at looking for signs of life began a few days later. No sign of anything to

Watching the red planet. This is one of the first photos of Mars taken by Viking I *in 1976.*

indicate that there might be any life on Mars was found, not even organic molecules. *Viking 2* landed in September with the same results. Sadly, Sagan had to give up his hope of finding Martians.

The Writer

It's been said that when NASA got tired of investigating planets, Sagan gave up on NASA and turned to writing books. That's not completely true, but his newfound fame had him trying to teach, write, appear on television, supervise graduate students, continue with his own research, and answer fan mail, all at the same time.

The Cosmic Connection had established a pattern that Sagan used in most of his books: a collection of essays. The books can be read leisurely, essay by essay, rather than straight through. In his next book, *Other Worlds,* Sagan began what became another life-long quest—to help people recognize pseudoscience, or false science. At that time, for example, a writer named Erick Von Däniken had published a book demonstrating "proof" that astronauts from another world had come to Earth long ago.

Other Worlds was a very small book, with little in it that was thought provoking. It was almost as if Sagan was saving his major thinking for his next book, which was published in 1977.

The Dragons of Eden: Speculations on the Evolution of Human Intelligence dealt with the way intelligence developed in humans through history. But Sagan didn't leave out his first love; he related the growth in human intelligence to SETI. "Both the existence of . . . other civilizations and the nature of the messages they may be sending depend on the universality of the process of evolution of intelligence that has occurred on Earth."

Sagan appeared on the cover of *Newsweek* magazine—a great honor for any writer—when the book was awarded the Pulitzer Prize for best nonfiction of the year. Clearly, Carl Sagan had become a writer. Biographer William Poundstone, author of *Carl Sagan: A Life in the Cosmos,* wrote, "To someone who knows science, it is amazing how much Sagan leaves *out* of explanations. This is not dumbed-down science but the truest form of clarity.

Murmurs of Earth

In 1977, Sagan became involved in doing again what he had done on the Pioneer probes—sending a message to the universe from Earth. This time the message was to travel on the Voyager probes scheduled to be launched in 1977. The Voyagers would travel by Jupiter and Saturn, sending back many photographs and measurements, and then continue sending occasional messages as they neared the edge of the solar system.

Sagan gathered such friends as Frank Drake, an artist named Jon Lomberg, science writer Timothy Ferris, and Ann Druyan, a writer he had met

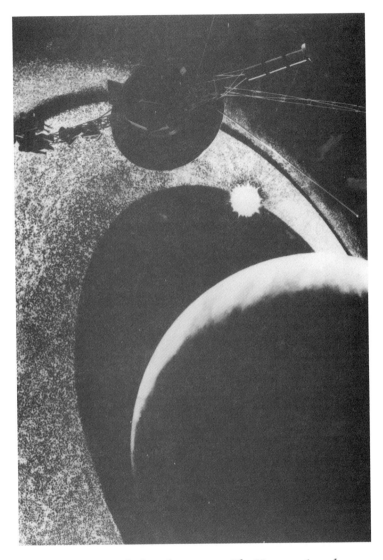

Communicating with the solar system. The Voyager 1 *probe carried information about Earth as it traveled to Jupiter and Saturn.*

through Ferris several years before. This time the group wanted to do more than just create a plaque. They wanted to send samples of Earth life, such as music, languages, maybe even art.

Arguing all the time about what would best represent the peoples of Earth, they finally put together a phonograph record that contained both sounds and images translated into electronic code. It included classical music, pop star Chuck Berry, jazz, and folksongs. It even included a human laugh—Carl Sagan's laugh—and the sounds of brain activity—Ann Druyan's.

All of this material was recorded on two copper disks, plated with gold. One disk was mounted on each Voyager craft. Of course, the arguments about their selections began the moment the list of contents was published in newspapers. Everyone had an opinion. Ethnic groups were angry at being omitted. There should be more women. There should be fewer women. Are enough items of African culture included?

In answer to these arguments, the group published a book called *Murmurs of Earth,* which described the process they went through in making their selections. Each person involved contributed an essay about the choices and explained his or her point of view.

In the middle of the twenty-first century, the Voyager craft will finally leave the influence of our sun and begin to wander through space, driven by the pushes and pulls of the stars. Perhaps, thousands of years from now, they will be found by a distant civilization and the "murmurs of Earth" will be heard.

Billions of stars. Sagan enjoyed hosting Cosmos, *a popular television series.*

COSMOS

4

arl Sagan was always disappointed when the public seemed uninterested in other planets unless scientists could show that there was life on them. This was especially true when the Viking landers were on Mars in 1976, and the newspapers paid little attention. That was when he realized that television could have a very important impact in the future. He could use this medium to help the public get excited about science.

Sagan and two other planetary scientists, Bruce Murray and Louis Friedman, founded the Planetary Society in 1980 to encourage the exploration of our solar system and the search for extraterrestrial life.

Because the public joined in large numbers, the society has had an important influence in bringing public opinion to government planners. The headquarters were established in Pasadena, California, and Sagan was the first president. Actor Paul Newman was one of the first contributors to the new organization. In 1985, the society started funding private efforts at SETI.

Much of the excitement that members brought to the new organization was generated by another Carl Sagan project. This time, he brought his world of astronomy directly to the public.

Making a TV Series

The new project began when Carl Sagan and B. Gentry Lee, a Viking mission-planning director, formed a company to produce science-based TV programs. Their goal was to bring science to the public in an interesting and entertaining manner. When television station KCET in Los Angeles, California, agreed to produce a series on astronomy in thirteen parts, Sagan, Lee, and the station producers all agreed that the series should "engage the heart as well as the mind."

The series was "dedicated to the proposition that the public is far more intelligent than it has generally been given credit for; that the deepest scientific questions on the nature and origin of the world excite the interests and passions of enormous numbers of people." In his introductory remarks to *Cosmos,* Sagan says, "Humans have evolved to wonder."

In making *Cosmos*, Sagan joined director Adrian Malone and the production crew to travel the world over. They wanted to take audiences to the places where things actually happened in the history of science. If they couldn't take them there, they made places look as if they were real. For instance, they used a model of the Viking lander on the dry surface of Death Valley in California, pretending they were on Mars.

They also used all the special effects available at the time (far fewer than the special effects now done by computers). Special effects had the attractive young astronomer sliding down a black hole and walking through a human brain, with electrical impulses flashing all around him. He also walked through the great library of ancient Alexandria, Egypt, which had been destroyed in the third century A.D.

On Sunday, September 28, 1980, American television audiences heard Dr. Carl Sagan's dramatic voice say, "The cosmos is all that is or ever was or ever will be." Those were the first words of the series that during the next few years was seen by 500 million people in sixty countries.

Until the PBS series *The Civil War,* which was directed by Ken Burns and aired in 1991, Sagan's *Cosmos* was the most-watched documentary TV series ever. It won an Emmy Award for the best documentary as well as the highly respected Peabody Award for television journalism.

In the years after the success of *Cosmos,* comedians could get a laugh just by saying "billions and billions." Sagan had gained a reputation for using that phrase many times during the series. But actually he never said it!

However, he used the phrase for the title of his last book, published after his death. As he explained at the beginning of *Billions and Billions: Thoughts on Life and Death at the Brink of the*

Sagan and Druyan in 1985. Many believed that his marriage to Ann Druyan was the best thing that ever happened to Carl Sagan.

Millennium, "I never said it. Honest. . . . for one thing, it's too imprecise. How many billions *are* 'billions and billions'?"

Annie

An influential person in the development of *Cosmos* was Ann Druyan, who had been involved in the *Murmurs of Earth* project. At the time of the launch of the Voyager probes, Carl and Linda Sagan had agreed to divorce. During the making of *Cosmos,* Sagan fell in love with Druyan, who was involved in all stages of production of the series. She was often credited with having the ability to calm down the two big egos of the production—Carl Sagan's and Adrian Malone's—when they argued.

Sagan and Druyan celebrated the success of the TV series by getting married in Los Angeles in June 1981. For the first time, apparently, Sagan was able to give his wife equal status in their marriage. Even Sagan's first wife, Lynn Margulis, and his first son, Dorion, agreed that Ann Druyan was the "best thing that ever happened to him." They would later have two children—another son, Sam, and Sagan's only daughter, Alexandra, called Sasha.

Cosmos the Book

Carl Sagan's book entitled *Cosmos* was published in 1980. Though based on the TV series, the book was not just a remake of the television show. It went into many subjects more deeply than could be done on TV. Also, Sagan was able to put personal notes in the book that were not appropriate on the television series.

The type of thing the book did well, which wouldn't have worked on TV, is an imaginary "captain's log" of the Voyager journeys to and around Jupiter, showing the photos relayed back to Earth and discoveries made. On Day 662, the captain writes, "We are free of Jupiter at last and sail again the sea of space. . . . Next port of call, two years hence: the Saturn system."

The book was a completely new experience. Even people who had seen the TV series several times found much new and exciting material in the book. It was on the *New York Times* best-seller list for seventy weeks and became the best-selling book on a science subject ever published in English. Together, the book and the TV series turned Carl Sagan into a worldwide celebrity.

The "Popularizer"

Unfortunately, his new status as Sagan-the-celebrity made life difficult for Sagan-the-scientist. Some of his colleagues expected him to stop doing any serious work. Others questioned whether he had *ever* done any serious work. They called him a "science popularizer," as if it were an insult, a terrible put-down.

Sagan has always felt it was imperative that the public understand science. Many decisions that affect our well-being as individuals and nations are in the hands of scientists. We must understand, as well as we can, what they are doing and why. If we don't understand what they are doing, we can't stop them making changes that can harm our future.

The public tends to assume that scientists are always objective—able to view the world around them without the personal likes and dislikes that most people have. But that is not always the case. However, we would not know that unless we make some attempt to understand what they are doing. Carl Sagan knew how important such understanding is, and he did not mind being labeled a "popularizer" by his colleagues.

Sagan on Cosmos. *Some people criticized the scientist's popularity and his appeal to the general public.*

Using His Celebrity

Keay Davidson, in his biography *Carl Sagan: A Life,* described the results of the TV series and book this way: "*Cosmos* gave Sagan the muscle to do bold new things: to sell a multimillion-dollar novel to Hollywood, to single-handedly save NASA's SETI project from congressional budget-cutters, to launch a privately funded SETI program—and to try to save the world from nuclear war."

That's pretty grand stuff, but it all came true. Sagan was able to use his newfound fame to do some of the things that meant the most to him.

His persuasiveness with Senator Proxmire saved the SETI budget. The private program was started with another bit of persuasiveness. Sagan persuaded moviemaker Steven Spielberg to donate $100,000 to start up a private SETI project. It set in motion the long-term use of an old radiotelescope at Harvard University.

Contact

The multimillion-dollar novel to which Keay Davidson referred was *Contact,* which was really another approach to SETI. The publisher gave Sagan a $2-million contract for the book in 1981. Up to that time, it was the largest amount ever paid for a book that had not yet been written.

Contact features a woman who had to overcome male prejudice to become a radioastronomer. She continues to confront that same prejudice when she becomes the first person to discover signals from space that indicate Earth is in contact with an extraterrestrial intelligence. At the end, in a fictional 1999, she makes a journey in a spacecraft that the extraterrestrial intelligence had directed Earthlings to build, raising questions about the universe itself.

The book was published in 1985 and immediately became a best-seller despite very mixed reviews. At the same time, another new Sagan book was selling. It was *Comet,* written with his wife, Ann. The book marked the first time that many readers learned what role comets might play in the origin of life.

Trying to Save the World

Sagan said, "The flip side of not finding life on another planet is appreciating life on Earth." This "flip side"—along with his wife Ann's encouragement—turned the space astronomer into a dedicated environmentalist.

Speaking out about nuclear winter. Sagan and other scientists warned that nuclear war could destroy the planet's environment.

One of the questions asked by Sagan and his colleagues in SETI was how long a civilization on another planet would last, and, thus, what would make it end. He feared that civilization on Earth might end as a result of nuclear war.

In 1983, Sagan co-authored a scientific article that started people talking about the idea of "nuclear winter." Called the TTAPS study (from the initials of the last names of its authors—R. P. Turco, O. B. Toon, T. P. Ackerman, J. B. Pollack, and Carl Sagan), it brought to public attention the idea that a nuclear war wasn't something that could be over and done with in a short period of time. Instead, it could destroy the environment that makes life possible on our planet.

The TAPPS study showed that a nuclear war would destroy the protective ozone layer in the stratosphere. In addition, the thick smoke and dust in the atmosphere from burning cities would block sunlight from reaching the planet's surface. Nuclear winter would begin. Even a few weeks of freezing temperatures and minimal sunlight would be enough to kill most living things on the planet.

This is the same climate change that scientists now think was responsible for the end of the Age of Dinosaurs about 65 million years ago. It has been accepted since 1980 that a meteor or asteroid struck Earth, probably in the Yucatan Peninsula of Mexico. The impact was so great and set so many forest fires that a shield of particles formed in the upper atmosphere. Sunlight was prevented from striking Earth's surface, and the planet cooled enough to kill the large beasts that depended on plant life to live. It was an "asteroid winter."

The idea of nuclear winter, if it was correct, showed that even a small war would set enough cities on fire to ultimately destroy the environment of the whole planet. Up until that time, President Ronald Reagan and many other high government officials thought that a "small" nuclear war could be "won." The scientists did not think that anyone could win.

Several years later, Soviet leader Mikhail Gorbachev began to make overtures to Washington, D.C., to end the long, expensive Cold War between the United States and the Soviet Union. Some people think that if the nuclear winter concept had not been made public (with people paying attention because it had Sagan's name on it), Washington might not have paid any attention to Gorbachev. And, in the long run, the Soviet Union might not have collapsed when it did in 1989.

In 1990, Sagan and Richard Turco (the T in TAPPS, and inventor of the term *nuclear winter*), published *A Path Where No Man Thought: Nuclear Winter and the End of the Arms Race*. The book described the discovery of nuclear winter and the political and scientific activity that resulted. Despite the awfulness of the things described, the book is hopeful. The title comes from the last words in the book: "There is reason to hope that, in our time also, there is a way out—a path where no man thought."

Much to say. Throughout his life, Sagan reached the public with his writing as well as his television appearances.

WRITER TO THE END

Years after the Voyager craft had taken their fantastic photographs of Jupiter and Saturn, Sagan encouraged NASA to send signals to the craft to make it turn around and take a picture of Earth. Because NASA didn't want the sun to burn out the craft's camera lenses, they waited until 1990 when the craft was already past Pluto and leaving the solar system.

The resulting pictures showed the inner planets of the solar system as a visitor from another world might see them. Earth itself appeared as a pale blue dot against the black sky. Sagan noted, "The Earth is a very small stage in a vast cosmic arena." He said this in *Pale Blue Dot: A Vision of the Human Future in Space,* the book he wrote in response to the sight. Published in 1994, he regarded it as a sequel to *Cosmos.* It updates and expands the material, concentrating on the planetary worlds that might be homes for future Earthlings.

At the same time, Sagan was dealing with Jupiter. Since childhood, he had been fascinated by this odd man out in the solar system—huge, gaseous, the center of a solar system of its own because it has at least sixteen moons in orbit around it. In the last years of his life, Sagan worked as a mission scientist once again, helping to plan the *Galileo* probe that would descend into Jupiter's atmosphere.

On October 18, 1989, *Galileo* was sent on its way from Earth orbit by the space shuttle *Atlantis.* On July 13, 1995, as it neared the giant planet, it separated into two parts. An orbiter entered Jupiter's orbit to act as a relay for signals from the probe, which plunged into the atmosphere. On December 7, 1995, the *Galileo* probe became the first Earth vehicle to enter the atmosphere of a giant planet. It encountered atmospheric pressure 230 times that of

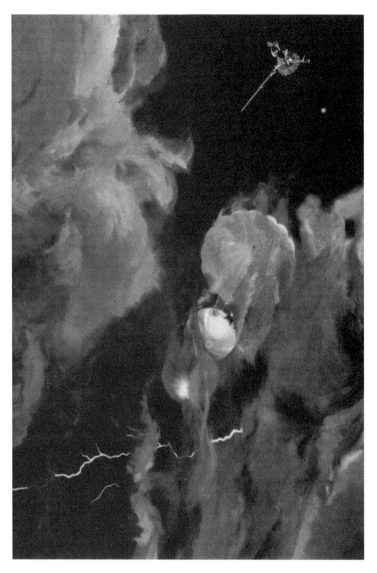

Galileo in 1995. This probe was the first spacecraft to enter Jupiter's atmosphere.

Earth. It transmitted data for almost an hour before being destroyed by the fierce temperatures.

Times of Disappointment

Sagan was proposed for membership in the prestigious 150-year-old National Academy of Sciences (NAS) in 1992. In what was supposed to be a secret vote but became known to the public, he was rejected. Many scientists felt that Sagan deserved to be recognized by membership of the NAS. But even more must have felt that he was more "popularizer" than scientist. Ironically, Sagan's first wife, Lynn Margulis, was already a member of NAS. She thought he should be accepted for membership. Keay Davidson wrote that perhaps Sagan "had become too famous for his own good."

Biologist Jared Diamond, writing later in *Discover* magazine, noted that Carl Sagan's experience of being rejected by his colleagues because he wrote for the public may result in young scientists being unwilling to bring their work to public understanding. He wrote, "Yet it is especially important for young scientists to be effective communicators because they are the ones most active in research, least diverted by administrative responsibilities, and the best role models for young people."

Two years later, the NAS gave Sagan its highest award, the Public Welfare Medal, for "distinguished contributions in the application of science to the public welfare." This award read as follows: "Carl Sagan has been enormously successful in communicating the wonder and importance of science. His ability to capture the imagination of millions and to explain difficult concepts in understandable terms is a magnificent achievement."

In 1993, the government ended its financial support of SETI. Fortunately, some of the people who were most fascinated by SETI were becoming wealthy in the computer and software businesses of Silicon Valley in California. Their companies provided the funding to establish Project Phoenix, run by the SETI Institute, which is now located in Mountain View, California.

Since 1999, any person in the world with a computer and a modem has been able to participate in SETI. A program headquartered at the University of California at Berkeley, called SETI@home, has sent small chunks of data recorded at Arecibo to home computers. The chunks are analyzed by a program provided and then returned to headquarters. Work is being done at a speed that would never have been possible before. Perhaps intelligent signals will be found.

Films, Celebrations, and Demons

Lynda Obst, an old friend of Ann Druyan's, had become a movie producer in Hollywood. She wanted to make a film of Sagan's novel *Contact*, but it took more than a decade for everyone to agree on how it should be done.

The *Contact* script was difficult to write. A movie that includes the philosophy and ideas expressed in a book is often boring. Questions of religion, feminism, and scientific accuracy had to be worked out.

The radioastronomer character, Ellie Arroway, had to be believable both as a lovely woman and a serious scientist. That was achieved when the very popular, talented, and intelligent Jodie Foster agreed to play the role.

As Sagan's sixtieth birthday approached, Cornell University organized a symposium—a conference at which many different people speak—to celebrate the occasion. More than 300 colleagues, fans, and friends attended to hear twenty-four different papers. They covered the exploration of planets, life

Jodie Foster in Contact. *The film was released the summer after Sagan's death.*

in the cosmos, science education, and public policy. The papers they read were gathered in a book called *Carl Sagan's Universe,* edited by Yervant Terzian, his boss at Cornell, and Elizabeth Bilson.

During the symposium, some of his friends noticed that Sagan did not look well. Within a few weeks, he was diagnosed with a very rare and serious disease that affected his bone marrow, the material in the middle of bone where blood cells are produced. A transplant of bone marrow from someone with compatible blood was his only chance for survival. The only possible donor was his sister Cari. She gladly went through the painful procedure—twice—during the following two years.

Each time it looked as if Sagan would beat the terrible disease, but then he became seriously ill again and was forced to return to the hospital in Seattle, Washington, where he was treated. Whenever he felt well, however, he continued to write, speak, and speculate.

The Demon-Haunted World: Science as a Candle in the Dark was published in 1996. This was a further explanation of the way people can avoid getting caught up in pseudoscience, such as UFOs, astrology, and ancient astronauts. He asked the readers to use the tools scientists use to check the soundness of a new idea. For example, just because an idea has not been disproved, does not mean that it's true. Or, all evidence must be used in reaching a decision, not just evidence that supports the belief. As Sagan often said, especially about SETI, "Absence of evidence is not evidence of absence."

Discoveries at the End

Even as he was seriously ill, Sagan never stopped paying attention to what astronomers were doing.

For example, in the 1990s, a meteorite—a rock from space that made it through Earth's atmosphere—was finally examined at Johnson Space Flight Center in Houston, Texas. This meteorite had been found some years before in Antarctica.

The "brownish potato," as Sagan described it, came from Mars. Its chemistry was closely studied, and it was found to contain microscopic structures that resemble the fossils of colonies of bacteria on Earth. Newspapers picked up "life on Mars" headlines once again.

Always thinking. In spite of illness, Sagan continued to work near the end of his life.

Sagan would like to have claimed that the discovery proved that there had once been life on Mars, but, as he had said about UFOs, "extraordinary claims require extraordinary evidence. The evidence for life on Mars is not yet extraordinary enough."

The very fact that scientists continually made SETI efforts implied that there were planets around other stars where civilizations had developed. But Earthlings had never proved that there were, in fact, planets around other stars. Then, in late 1995, Alex Wolszczan, a scientist at Penn State University, located—for certain—the very first new planetary system found to orbit another star. The star is a pulsar, the remains of a star that once blew itself up into a supernova.

Soon after Wolszczan's discovery, astronomers at San Francisco State University reliably identified planets around some other stars that are more like our sun. Most of the planets discovered seem to be like Jupiter—giant gaseous planets.

Sagan had always thought that planetary systems must be fairly common throughout the universe. He marveled about these exciting discoveries in *Billions and Billions* and suggested that many more would be coming soon. Perhaps the searchers will find "a few small blue worlds graced with water oceans, oxygen atmospheres, and the telltales signs of wondrous life."

Dr. Carl Sagan's own wondrous life ended on December 20, 1996. He died in a hospital with members of all three families around him. Vice President Al Gore wrote to Ann Druyan, "It is appropriate that the man who wrote the *Encyclopaedia Britannica* entry on 'Life' should have taught us all so much about living."

Mars and Memorials

On July 4, 1997, Mars Pathfinder landed on Mars, thirty years after the first flyby of the planet. After the successful landing, protected by airbag, the lander opened up and a small roving unit called *Sojourner* crawled out to explore the surface. Its information and photographs were relayed back to Earth by the lander. When NASA was certain that Pathfinder was successful, the lander was renamed the Sagan Memorial Station in his honor. The astronomer will forever be on Mars.

Interest in Mars has grown again, though not all the space missions have been successful. A Mars

On the surface. In 1997, Mars Pathfinder landed on Mars and was later named the Sagan Memorial Station.

Observer exploded in 1993. A Mars Polar Lander was expected to search for water on Mars after landing in the region near a pole. However, communication was lost before it had even landed on the planet in December 1999.

Much more successful was the Mars Global Surveyor. By the end of the year 2000, it had sent more than 60,000 images of the planet back to Earth to be used in making an accurate map.

Carl Sagan: Astronomer

In October 2000, NASA announced that there would be perhaps six Mars missions during the coming decade, with rock samples brought back to Earth by 2011. Many of these missions are being planned by scientists who were once Carl Sagan's students.

Mars Odyssey is scheduled to land on the planet in 2001. Perhaps in memory of Carl Sagan, who tried to get such an instrument on an earlier flight, Mars Odyssey will carry a microphone to transmit to Earth the sounds made by the winds of Mars.

Even after his death, Sagan's work lives on. The American Astronomical Society's Division of Planetary Sciences created the Carl Sagan Medal to honor work in the spirit of Sagan—excellence in communicating planetary science to the public. It was given in 1998 for the first time, to astronomer, author, and space artist William Hartmann, a senior scientist at the Planetary Science Institute in Tucson, Arizona.

The Sciencenter, a museum in Ithaca, New York, created an imaginative memorial to Dr. Sagan in downtown Ithaca—a miniature solar system that a person can walk through. The Sagan Planet Walk starts with the sun, and a visitor can choose how far to go into the accurately proportioned solar system—to nearby Mercury, a slightly longer jaunt to

Venus, or—for the energetic—a ten-minute hike to Pluto.

The most widespread memorial to Carl Sagan was the film *Contact*, which was released the summer after his death. Like the author's life, the reviews were mixed.

A Candle in the Dark

Sagan himself summarized what had been accomplished in astronomy, just during his own career, in the 1992 issue of *The Planetary Report*, published by the Planetary Society:

> *We humans have sent robots, then animals and then ourselves above the blue skies of Earth into the black interplanetary void. The footprints of 12 of us are scattered across the lunar surface, where they will last a million years. We have flown by some 60 new worlds, many of them discovered in the process. Our ships have set gently down on scorching Venus and chilly Mars, returning images of their surfaces and searching for life. Once above our blanket of air, we have turned our telescopes into the depths of space and back on our small planet to see it all as one*

A man remembered. Carl Sagan will long be regarded as a driving force in space exploration and environmental protection.

interconnected and interdependent whole. We have launched artificial moons and artificial planets, and we have sent four spacecraft on their way to the stars. . . If we manage to avoid self-destruction, so that there are future historians, our time will be remembered in part because this was when we first set sail for other worlds.

Yervant Terzian, Sagan's boss at Cornell University, said, "He was, quite simply, the best science educator in the world this century. Carl was a candle in the dark."

TIMELINE

1934 Carl Sagan born in Brooklyn, New York, on November 9

1945 Moves with his family to Rahway, New Jersey

1951 Graduates from high school and enrolls at the University of Chicago

1956 Enters the University of Chicago graduate program in astronomy; delivers his first scientific paper

1957 Marries Lynn Alexander

1960 Earns his Ph.D. in astronomy and physics

1961 Begins working for the Institute for Basic Research in Science

1962 Divorces Lynn Alexander; begins working as an assistant professor at Harvard University

1966 With I. S. Shklovskii, publishes *Intelligent Life in the Universe*

1968 Becomes editor of *Icarus*; is denied tenure at Harvard; takes a professorship at Cornell University; marries Linda Salzman

1972	Helps create the message carried on *Pioneer 10*
1973	Publishes *The Cosmic Connection*; appears on *The Tonight Show* for the first time
1970s	Helps plan the Viking missions
1976	Begins working with others on message to be carried on Voyager probes; agrees to divorce Linda Salzman
1977	Publishes *The Dragons of Eden*, which wins him the Pulitzer Prize for nonfiction
1978	Speaks with Senator William Proxmire about SETI funding
1980	With two other scientists, founds the Planetary Society; begins hosting *Cosmos* TV series; publishes *Cosmos*, based on the TV show
1981	Marries Ann Druyan
1983	Co-authors article about nuclear winter
1985	Publishes *Contact* and, with Ann Druyan, *Comet*
1990	With Richard Turco, publishes *A Path Where No Man Thought*
1992	Is denied membership in the National Academy of Science (NAS)
1996	Publishes *The Demon-Haunted World*; dies on December 20
1997	The film *Contact* is released; *Billions and Billions* is published

HOW TO BECOME AN ASTRONOMER

The Job

Astronomers study the universe and all of its celestial bodies. They collect and analyze information about the moon, planets, sun, and stars, which they use to predict their shapes, sizes, brightness, and motions.

They are interested in the orbits of comets, asteroids, and even artificial satellites. Information on the size and shape, the luminosity and position, the composition, characteristics, and structure as well as temperature, distance, motion, and orbit of all celestial bodies is of great relevancy to their work.

Practical application of activity in space is used for a variety of purposes. The launching of space vehicles and satellites has increased the importance of the information astronomers gather. For example, the public couldn't enjoy the benefits of accurate predictions of weather as early if satellites weren't keeping an eye on our atmosphere. Without astronomical data, satellite placement wouldn't be possible. Knowledge of the orbit of planets and their moons, as well as asteroid activity, is also vital to astronauts exploring space.

Astronomers are usually expected to specialize in some particular branch of astronomy. The *astrophysicist* is concerned with applying the concepts of physics to stellar atmospheres and interiors. *Radio astronomers* study the source and nature of celestial radio waves, with extremely sensitive radio telescopes. The majority of astronomers either teach or do research or a combination of both. Astronomers in many universities are expected to teach such subjects as physics and mathematics in addition to astronomy. Other astronomers are engaged in such activities as the development of astronomical instruments, administration, technical writing, and consulting.

Astronomers who make observations may spend long periods of time in observatories. Astronomers who teach or work in laboratories may work eight-hour days. However, those who make observations, especially during celestial events or other peak viewing times may spend long evening hours in observatories. Paperwork is a necessary part of the job. For teachers, it can include lesson planning and paper grading. Astronomers conducting research independently or for a university can expect to spend a considerable amount of time writing grant proposals to secure funding for their work. For any scientist, sharing the knowledge acquired is a vital part of the work.

Astronomers are expected to painstakingly document their observations and eventually combine them into a coherent report, often for peer review or publication.

Although the telescope is the major instrument used in observation, many other devices are also used by astronomers in carrying out these studies, including spectrometers for the measurement of wavelengths of radiant energy, photometers for the measurement of light intensity, balloons for carrying various measuring devices, and computers for processing and analyzing all the information gathered.

Astronomers use ground-based telescopes for night observation of the skies. The Hubble Space Telescope, which magnifies the stars at a much greater percentage than land-based capability allows, has become an important tool for the work of many astronomers.

Requirements

High School While in high school, all prospective astronomers should take mathematics (including analytical geometry and trigonometry), science courses (including chemistry and physics), English, foreign languages, and courses in the humanities and social sciences. Students should also be well-grounded in the use of computers and in computer programming.

Postsecondary Training All astronomers are required to have some postsecondary training, with a doctoral degree being the usual educational requirements because most jobs are in research and development. A master's degree is sufficient for some jobs in applied research and development, and a bachelor's degree is adequate for some nonresearch jobs. Students should select a college program with wide offerings in physics, mathematics, and astronomy and should take as many of these courses as possible. Graduate training will normally take about three years beyond the bachelor's degree.

Bachelor's degrees in astronomy are offered by about 175 institutions in the United States, and 80 institutions offer master's or doctorates in the field. A sampling of the astronomy courses typically offered in graduate school are celestial mechanics, galactic structure, radio astronomy, stellar atmospheres and interiors, theoretical astrophysics, and binary and variable stars. Some graduate schools require that an applicant for a doctorate spend several months in residence at an observatory. In most institutions, the student's graduate courses will reflect his or her chosen astronomical specialty or particular field of interest.

Other Requirements

The field of astronomy calls for people with a strong but controlled imagination. They must be able to see relationships between what may appear to be, on the surface, unrelated facts, and they must be able to form various hypotheses regarding these relationships. Astronomers must be able to concentrate over long periods of time. They should also express themselves well both in writing and speaking.

Exploring

A number of summer or part-time jobs are usually available in observatories. The latter may be either on a summer or year-round basis. These jobs not only offer experience in astronomy but often act as stepping stones to good jobs upon graduation. Students employed in observatories might work as guides or as assistants to astronomers.

Students can test their interest in this field by working part-time, either as an employee or as a volunteer, in planetariums or science museums. Many people enjoy astronomy as a hobby, and there are a number of amateur astronomy clubs and groups active throughout the country. Amateur astronomers have often made important contributions to the field of astronomy. In 1996, for example, a new comet was discovered by an amateur astronomer in Japan. Students may gain experience in studying the skies by purchasing, or even building, their own telescopes.

Reading or using the Internet to learn more on your own is also a good idea. What about astronomy interests you? You can find specific information in books or on the Internet. Check out the National Aeronautics and Space Administration (NASA)'s Website at http://www.nasa.gov. It contains useful information about careers in astronomy and aeronautics and information about current space exploration. When you hear in the news that a comet or meteor shower will be visible from Earth, be sure to set your alarm to get up and watch and learn. Science teachers will often discuss such events in class.

Employers

About 55 percent of professionals in the earth and space sciences are employed by educational institutions, according to a 1998 employment survey by the Commission on Professionals in Science and Technology. Another 25 percent are employed by private industry and 18 percent are employed by the government.

Astronomers frequently find jobs as faculty members at colleges and universities or are affiliated with those institutions through observatories and laboratories. Roughly 20 percent of nonfaculty astronomers worked for commercial or noncommercial research, development, and testing laboratories in 1998, according to the U.S. Department of Labor. The federal government employs astronomers with agencies such as NASA, the U.S Naval Observatory, the Army Map Service, and the Naval Research Laboratory. Other astronomers work in planetariums, science museums, or other public service positions involved in presenting astronomy to the general public; teach physics or earth sciences in secondary schools; or are science journalists and writers.

In the private sector, astronomers are hired by consulting firms that supply astronomical talent to the government for specific tasks. In addition, a number of companies in the aerospace industry hire astronomers to work in related areas where they can use their background and talents in instrumentation, remote sensing, spectral observations, and computer applications.

Starting Out

A chief method of entry for astronomers with a doctorate is to register with the college's placement bureau, which provides contacts with one of the agencies looking for astronomers. Astronomers can also apply directly to universities, colleges, planetariums, government agencies, aerospace industry manufacturers, and others who hire astronomers. Many positions are advertised in professional and scientific journals devoted to astronomy and astrophysics.

Graduates with bachelor's or master's degrees can normally obtain semiprofessional positions in observatories, planetariums, or some of the larger colleges and universities offering training in astronomy. Their work assignments might be as research assistants, optical workers, observers, or technical assistants. Those employed by colleges or universities might well begin as instructors. Federal government positions in astronomy are usually earned on the basis of competitive examinations given periodically by the Board of United States Civil Service Examiners for Scientific and Technical Personnel. Jobs with some municipal organizations employing astronomers are often based on competitive examinations. The examinations are usually open to those with bachelor's degrees.

NASA offers internships for students with some postsecondary training. To find out more about NASA internships and other opportunities, explore the Website at *http://www.nasajobs.nasa.gov.*

Advancement
Because of the relatively small size of the field, advancement may be somewhat limited. A professional position in a large university or governmental agency is often considered the most desirable post available to an astronomer because of the opportunities it offers for

additional study and research. Those employed in a college may well advance from instructor to assistant professor to associate professor and then to professor. There is also the possibility of eventually becoming a department head.

Opportunities also exist for advancement in observatories or industries employing people in astronomy. In these situations, as in those in colleges and universities, advancement depends to a great extent on the astronomer's ability, education, and experience. Peer recognition, in particular for discoveries that broaden the understanding of the field, is often a determinant of advancement. Publishing articles in professional journals, such as *Scientific American* or the *American Journal of Astrophysics* is a way for astronomers to become known and respected in the field. Advancement isn't usually speedy; an astronomer may spend years devoted to a specific research problem before being able to publish conclusions or discoveries in a scientific journal.

Earnings

In educational institutions, salaries are normally regulated by the salary schedule prevailing in that particular institution. As the astronomer advances to higher-level teaching positions, his or her salary increases significantly. According to a 1998 survey by the Commission on Professionals in Science and Technology, professionals holding doctoral degrees in earth and space sciences averaged $33,000 for nine-month contracts in educational institutions. Salaries for space professionals in business and industry were higher, with an average salary of $58,600.

Another survey, conducted by the National Association of Colleges and Employers, focused on professionals who hold physics doctoral degrees, which covers many astronomers. According to the 1999 survey, the average starting salary offered to physics doctoral candidates was $60,300. The American Institute of Physics reported a median salary of $70,000 in 1998 for its members with Ph.D.s; $57,000 for master's degree professionals; and $54,000 for those with bachelor's degrees. The average for space professionals employed by the federal government in 1999 was $81,300, according to the U.S. Department of Labor.

Opportunities also exist in private industry for well-trained and experienced astronomers, who often find their services in demand as consultants. Fees for this type of work may run as high as $200 per day in some of the more specialized fields of astronomy.

Work Environment

Astronomers' activities may center on the optical telescope. Most telescopes are located high on a hill or mountain and normally in a fairly remote area where the air is clean and the view is not affected by lights from unrelated sources. There are some 300 of these observatories in the United States.

Astronomers working in these observatories usually are assigned to observation from three to six nights per month and spend the remainder of their time in an office or laboratory where they study and analyze their data. They also must prepare reports. They may work with others on one segment of their research or writing and then work entirely alone on the next. Their work is normally carried on in clean, quiet, well-ventilated, and well-lighted facilities.

Those astronomers in administrative positions, such as director of an observatory or planetarium, will maintain fairly steady office hours but may also work during the evening and night. They usually are more involved in administrative details, however, and not so much in observation and research.

Those employed as teachers will usually have good facilities available to them, and their hours will vary according to class hours assigned. Work for those employed by colleges and universities may often be more than forty hours per week.

Outlook

Little change is expected in the growth rate in this field through 2008 according to the U.S. Department of Labor. Astronomy is one of the smallest science fields, employing fewer than 4,000 people in the mid-1990s, according to the *Princeton Review*. Currently, there are about 150 openings each year for professional astronomers. These result from the normal turnover when workers retire or leave the field for other reasons. Competition for these jobs, particularly among new people entering the profession, will continue to be strong. In recent years, the number of new openings in this field have not kept pace with the number of astronomers graduating from the universities, and this trend is likely to continue for the near future.

The federal government will continue to provide employment opportunities for astronomers. However, government agencies, particularly NASA, may find their budgets reduced in the coming years, and the number of new positions created for astronomers will likely drop as well. Few new observatories will be constructed, and those currently in existence are not expected to greatly increase the size of their staffs.

The greatest growth in employment of astronomers is expected to occur in business and industry. Companies in the aerospace field will need more astronomers to do research that will help them develop new equipment and technology.

TO LEARN MORE ABOUT ASTRONOMERS

Books

Fox, Mary Virginia. *Edwin Hubble: American Astronomer.* Danbury, Conn.: Franklin Watts, 1997.

Hightower, Paul W. *Galileo: Astronomer and Physicist.* Springfield, N.J.: Enslow, 1997.

Hinman, Bonnie. *Benjamin Banneker: American Mathematician and Astronomer.* Broomall, Penn.: Chelsea House, 2000.

Websites

The American Association of Amateur Astronomers
http://www.corvus.com/
For information about all kinds of amateur activities

Astronomy.com
http://www.astronomy.com/home.asp
For the latest news about the field of astronomy

Astronomy Now Online
http://www.astronomynow.com
For information about current astronomy events

Where to Write
American Astronomical Society
2000 Florida Avenue, Suite 400
Washington, DC 20009
Email: aas@aas.org
For information that concerns today's astronomers

American Institute of Physics
1 Physics Ellipse
College Park, MD 20740-3843
Email: aipinfo@aip.org
A resource for professionals who work in many physics
disciplines, including astronomy

NASA
http://www.nasa.gov/
To learn all about this organization and its current projects

TO LEARN MORE ABOUT CARL SAGAN

Books

Byman, Jeremy. *Carl Sagan: In Contact with the Cosmos.* Greensboro, N.C.: Morgan Reynolds, 2000.

Cohen, Daniel. *Carl Sagan: Superstar Scientist.* New York: Putnam, 1987.

Schwarts, Joyce R., and Ellen R. Butts. *Carl Sagan.* A&E Biography. Minneapolis: Lerner, 2000.

Websites

Carl Sagan Productions
http://www.carlsagan.com
Information about Sagan's work along with lists of important links

The Planetary Society: Carl Sagan Tribute
http://www.planetary.org/society/tributes/index.html
A biography of Sagan, the society's founder

World Socialist Web Site/Carl Sagan (1934–1996): An Appreciation

http://www.wsws.org/science/1997/jan1997/saganj13.shtml
Biographical information about Sagan as well as his views on science, history, reason, and thought

Interesting Places to Visit

Arecibo Observatory
Route 625
Bo Esperanza
Arecibo, Puerto Rico 00612
787/878-2612
To tour the world's largest single-disk radiotelescope

Cornell University
Information and Referral Center
Day Hall Lobby
Ithaca, New York 14853-2801
607/254-4636
To visit the university where Sagan taught for many years; also worth seeing is the Fuertes Observatory (phone: 607/225-3557)

Hayden Planetarium
Rose Center for Earth and Space
American Museum of Natural History
West 81st Street at Central Park West
New York, NY 10024
212/769-5100
To see where Sagan got his early inspiration

Sciencenter
Sagan Planet Walk
601 First Street
Ithaca, NY 14850
607/272-0600
607/277-7469 (fax)
info@sciencenter.org
To see a scale model of the solar system

INDEX

Page numbers in *italics* indicate illustrations.

ABOUT THE AUTHOR

Jean Blashfield has written about ninety books, most of them for young people. She likes best to write about interesting places, but she loves history and science too. In fact, one of her big advantages as a writer is that she becomes fascinated by just about every subject she investigates. She has created an encyclopedia of aviation and space, written popular books on murderers and house plants, and had a lot of fun creating an early book on the things women have done, called *Hellraisers, Heroines, and Holy Women.*

In Wisconsin, she delighted in finding TSR, Inc., the publishers of the *Dungeons & Dragons* games. At that company, she founded a new department to publish fantasy gamebooks and novels, and helped the company expand into a worldwide enterprise.

Ms. Blashfield lives in Delavan, Wisconsin.